Bustling
CITIES
of the World

ALBATROS

Travel
around the world's

Reykjavík ....

Vancouver

New Orleans

New York

London

Paris

Santa Fe 56

58

52

San Francisco .....

54

50

Miami

Barcelona

Lisbon

60

Mexico City ......

62

Rio de Janeiro

N

W — E

S

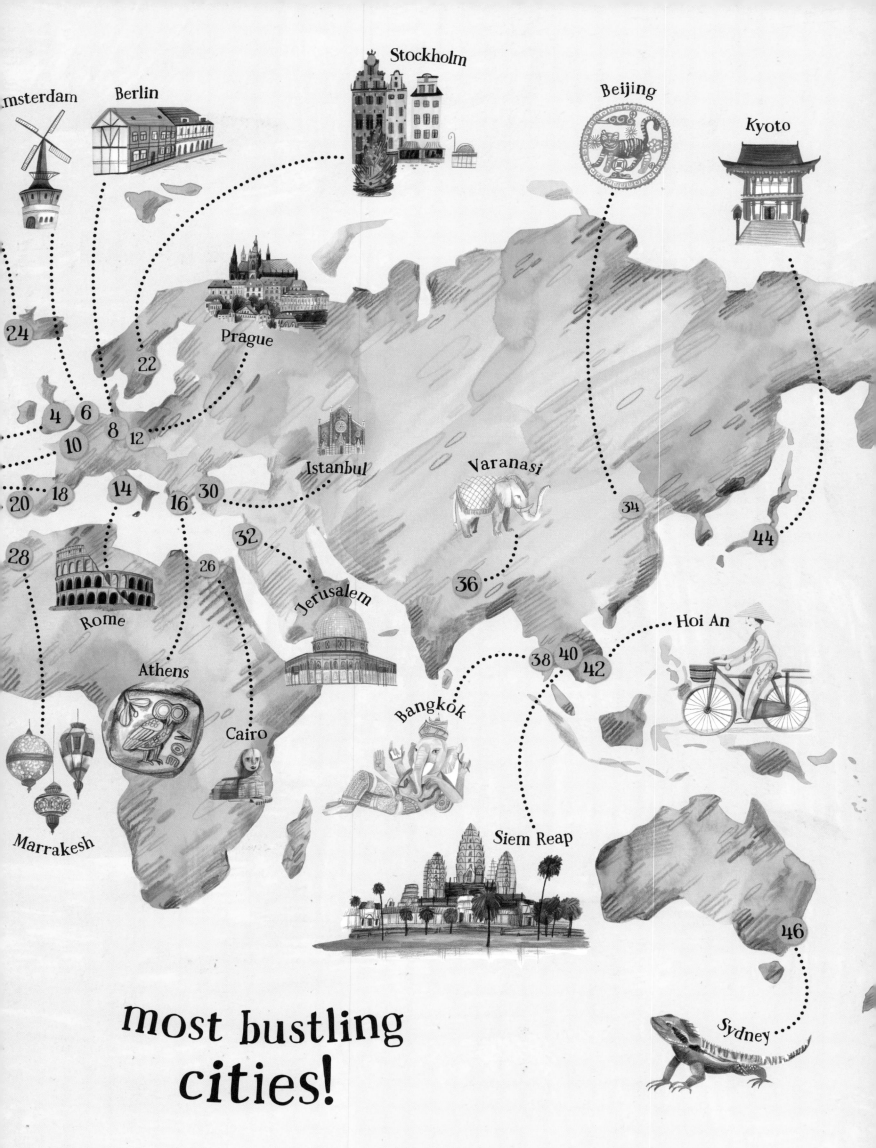

Amsterdam

Berlin

Stockholm

Beijing

Kyoto

24

Prague

22

4   6

8

10   12

18   14

20   16   30

28

32

26

Istanbul

Varanasi

34

36

44

Rome

Jerusalem

Hoi An

Athens

38 40

42

Cairo

Bangkok

Marrakesh

Siem Reap

46

Sydney

most bustling
cities!

LONDON

It's raining again—no surprise to Londoners. Nobody leaves home without a hat, cap, or umbrella—just look at Sherlock Holmes, a palace guard, even the Queen! But if you do get wet, don't despair—you'll warm up nicely at the traditional five o'clock tea.

London taxi

Queen's Guard

London police

Big Ben

umbrella

double-decker bus

Palace of Westminster

The Gherkin

The Shard

Nelson's column

British Museum

Globe Theatre

William Shakespeare

Queen Elizabeth II

Charlie Chaplin

Sherlock Holmes

Oliver Twist

corgis

London Eye

The Sunday Times newspaper

The Times

gray squirrel

Hyde Park

10 Downing Street

10

Francis Drake's ship

raincoat

red telephone booth

TELEPHONE

stables in Wimbledon district

Wimbledon tennis championship

cricket

fish and chips

wellington boots

Westminster Abbey

five o'clock tea

Scotch egg

cookies

London pie

Tower Bridge

St Paul's Cathedral

THE TUBE

London Underground

5

Vincent's Starry Night

Piet Mondrian

Pancake Boat

Vincent van Gogh

Maritime Museum

Girl with a Pearl Earring

Amsterdam street art

Anne Frank

EYE Filmmuseum

Muiden Castle

Anne Frank House

Rijksmuseum

canal

Jordaan district

Torensluis bridge

Tulip festival

bicycles

Dutch fries

mint tea

Bitterballen meatballs

caramel

waffle

Poffertjes pancakes

Dutch eel

Amsterdam Centraal Station

NEMO Science Museum

De Gooyer windmill

historical buildings alongside the River Amstel

flower market

world's largest flea market

paternoster lift

AMSTERDAM

feeding goats in Park Centraal

Over bridges, across canals, or further still? In Amsterdam, you can ride your bicycle as fast as the pedals will power you. Take in the beauty of tulip fields in bloom, feel the wind in your hair and the seagulls squawking, and don't forget to check out the Van Gogh Museum for the famous painter's beloved sunflowers!

Keukenhof flower garden

Museumplein park

tulips

Albert **Einstein**

David Bowie

beer

hops

Königsberger
Klopse

Berlin
Television Tower

Berlin
Philharmonic

Museum Island

Currywurst

pretzel

East Side
Gallery

River
Spree

Gendarmenmarkt

Military
History
Museum

bear emblem

Berlin
Cathedral

Tempelhof
Airport

Victory Column

wild boar

Knut the polar bear

beer garden

Berliner Tuba

Berlin Wall

Berlin Botanical Garden

Little Traffic-light Man

Spandau

Copy of Ishtar Gates

Rixdorf

Oberbaum Bridge

Brandenburg Gate

S-Bahn urban rail system

electronic music

Classic Remise

BERLIN

Take a bite of a crunchy pretzel as you stroll along the Berlin Wall—white concrete that once split Berlin in two. Fortunately, Berlin is one unified city again, and it's big enough for everyone, including the world's largest orchestra (128 musicians), as well as past residents like world-famous physicist Albert Einstein and Knut the polar bear.

Kreuzberg

Tiergarten park

Holocaust Memorial

Jewish Museum

Berlin Zoo

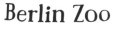

9

mime artist

the first balloons

Les Invalides

Jules Verne

Eiffel Tower

cats

Champs-Élysées

Arc de Triomphe

plane trees

peony

stethoscope

puppet theater

boulangerie

toy sailboats

magnolias

jambon-beurre baguette

croissant

Jardin du Palais-Royal

Paris Métro entrance

METROPOLITAIN

cheeses

escargots

macarons

street painter

Edgar Degas ballerinas

Claude Monet

Mona Lisa

Louvre

pétanque court

10

original street-name signs

RUE VERDI

perfumes

fashion

Coco Chanel

Edith Piaf

bob haircut

Le Chat Noir

TOURNÉE DU CHAT NOIR DE RODOLPHE SALIS

Alfons Mucha poster

PARIS

The smell of freshly roasted coffee, luxurious perfumes, and delicate pink peonies fill the air . . . Welcome to Paris, the city of fashion and art! Get yourself a custom-tailored suit, or have your portrait painted by a local artist for next to nothing. If your romantic stroll takes you to the Louvre Museum, you can meet the Mona Lisa, a charming painted lady who will surely wink and smile at you mysteriously. Oh Paris! Who could resist you?

Sacré-Cœur basilica

Parisian café

Le Dome

Montmartre

Cité florale

Moulin Rouge

MOULIN ROUGE

Art Nouveau streetlamp

merry-go-round

Notre-Dame cathedral

bouquiniste

love locks

street piano

11

Golden Lane

Prague Castle

St. Vitus Cathedral

alchemist

Charles Bridge

Václav Havel

Vltava River

Franz Kafka

Bedřich Smetana

Antonín Dvořák

beef sirloin

beer

Prague ham

tour boats

spit cake

marinated creamy cheese

squirrel

Czech puppets

Charles IV

open sandwiches

pork knuckle

roses

National Museum

St. Wenceslas

Municipal House

Powder Tower

Wenceslas Square

statue of St. Wenceslas

SVATÝ · VÁCLAVE

Petřín hill

lime tree

Vyšehrad fort

Letná hill

Žižkov Television Tower

Golem

Petřín Mirror Maze

PRAGUE

Stroll through the Golden Lane of this city of a hundred spires and you'll come across majestic figures from history—kings, composers, and even alchemists—but the most remarkable of all is the Golem, a manmade figure of clay who, legend has it, crosses Charles Bridge every night. His footsteps can be heard all the way up Petřín hill!

Old New Synagogue

Astronomical Clock

St. Nicholas Church

Troja Palace

cobblestones

Jewish cemeteries

Dancing House

Gingerbread museum

vintage car

National Theatre

John Lennon Wall

ALL YOU NEED IS LOVE FREEDOM TRUTH

Kampa island

13

giant foot

oranges

artichokes

black and white mosaics

spaghetti **carbonara**

ROME

Ancient Rome has a sacred atmosphere of days long past—as well it should. It was home to celebrated sculptors and orators, as well as eminent politicians like Julius Caesar. Today, it's the seat of the Pope. Let's explore this beautiful city—and maybe enjoy a scoop of icy sweet gelato along the way!

gelato

Colosseum

Roman numerals

LXVII XCVIIII

Via **Appia**

Pantheon

cypresses

Julius Caesar

Cicero the orator

Vespa

Roman pizza

maritozzi

Rome Rose **Garden**

14

Vatican City

St. Peter's Basilica

Pope Francis

Roman columns

Villa Borghese park

Orange Trees Garden

Roman aqueduct

St. Peter's Square

Caesar Augustus

Roman statues

Trevi Fountain

Forum Romanum

Trajan's Column

Capitoline Wolf

Trastevere neighbourhood

Romulus and Remus

Victor Emanuel II Monument

Socrates

Plato

souvlaki

dolmas

Greek salad

Ancient Greek pottery

Chapel of St. George

Hippocrates

Greek dancers

Mount Lycabettus

Arch of Hadrian

Monastiraki Square

silver coin from Athens

olives

ATHENS

We race through the streets of Athens in the footsteps of the Ancient Greeks—like Pheidippides, the famous marathon runner—running nimbly up and down the steps in the Odeon three times. We must be careful not to stumble; there's still a slalom around the columns of the Parthenon to complete! To treat a complicated ankle fracture, the Ancient Greek physician Hippocrates would surely recommend modern medicine.

Plaka neighborhood

hoplite helmet

amphora

16

goddess **Athena**

Parthenon

Icarus

Olive Tree of the Acropolis

Academy of Athens

Hadrian's **Library**

Daphni Monastery

Mask of Agamemnon

Porch of the Maidens at the Erechtheion

Medusa **mosaic**

Temple of Olympian Zeus

National Archeology Museum

Pheidippides

marathon run

kitharas **and lyre**

Port of Piraeus

Odeon amphitheater

17

colored tiles

BARCELONA

Ah, Barcelona—what a sight to behold!
From painted tiles to colorful mosaics to walls
that appear to be dancing, the streets are full of
vibrant sights that captivate the senses. Meanwhile,
there's a lot happening on the soccer fields, where
players run like the wind while the fans cry,
"Yay! Barcel-o-o-o-na!" All this cheering makes
them hungry, so after the game they head off for
classic dishes like tapas and paella.

bull

gardens filled
with cactuses

mosaics

Gothic
Quarter

flamenco

Sopa
de Galets

Sagrada
Família

La Barceloneta
beach

singing
Magic Fountain

18

Park Güell

cubism

Sagrat Cor

skateboarders

soccer

Palace of
Catalan Music

Arc de Triomf

street in
El Born quarter

tapas

paella

crema
Catalana

La Boqueria
market

Casa
Milá

La Rambla

Casa Batlló

19

piri-piri chicken

ginjinha

pastel de nata

Museu Nacional do Azulejo

octopus à lagareiro

amêijoas à bulhão pato

Museu da Filigrana

Feira da Ladra market

Sé Catedral de Lisboa

caldo verde

Seashell Gallery

fado music

Livraria Bertrand

Padrão dos Descobrimentos

Monasterio de los Jerónimos de Belém

sardines

Vasco da Gama

dos Marqueses de Fronteira

Palácio

bougainvillea

Carcavelos beach

Praça do Comércio

20

Castelo **de São Jorge**

Elevador da Bica

cork oak

cork handbag

Rossio square

Lisbon no. 28 tram

Cristo Rei

Alfama district

Lisbon Zoo

Aqueduto das Águas Livres

LISBON

"To Lisbon and beyond!" cries the famous explorer Vasco da Gama, stocking up on sardines and mussels before leaving on a long ocean voyage from Europe's westernmost capital. The Belém Tower's call echoes across the vast Atlantic Ocean, its azulejos—painted tin-glazed ceramic tilework—shimmering blue and white, beckoning him to undiscovered lands!

Basílica de Estrela

Belém Tower

Bordallo Pinheiro fountain

Ponte 25 de Abril

Pippi Longstocking

Nobel Prize

Greta Thunberg

SKOLSTREJK FÖR KLIMATET

Red Mill

ABBA
The Museum

Strandvägen waterfront

ghost walk

SkyView

Avicii Arena

Gamla Stan

City Hall

Old Seglora Church

Gröna Lund amusement park

Vasa maritime museum

Lake Mälaren

Vikingaliv runestone

Üto archipelago

model of Bullerbyn village

Skansen museum

22

Wooden Horse **Museum**

ice hockey

Scandinavian **design**

Järnpoike miniature statue

St James's Church

STOCKHOLM

Hidden beneath a mountain of snow, this place was first settled by the weather-beaten Vikings—quite the cozy place compared to the icy seas of the far North. Nowadays in Stockholm, you're likely to run into Pippi Longstocking. You can also skate on Lake Mälaren and follow it up with a must-have Swedish break—fika—for a cup of hot tea and a sweet snack.

Bergianska trädgården

Stortorget square

Rosendals **Trädgård**

Royal National City Park

Swedish Police on horseback

Swedish royal standard

fika

Swedish **sandwich cake**

royal crown of Sweden

Queen Christina's **Silver Throne**

salmon with dill sauce

armor from Stockholm Palace

smorgasbord

Mount Esja

Old Town

Northern Lights

polar fox

Blue Lagoon

statue of Ingólfr Arnarson

oldest house in Reykjavík

Imagine Peace Tower

Björk

lopapeysa

Perlan museum of Icelandic natural wonders

Hallgrímskirkja church

Saga Museum

Viking figurine

Harpa Concert Hall

fish and chips with mushy peas

fish soup

lamb

The Sun Voyager

runestones

National Gallery of Iceland

Icelandic meat soup

skyr

ice cream and cheese

rye bread

Tjörnin Lake

licorice

Mermaid statue

Viðey island

greylag goose

whooper swan

REYKJAVÍK

Snæfellsjökull glacier

reindeer

puffins

Volcano Show

volcanic rocks

Sky Lagoon

Snuggle up in a lopapeysa (a warm Icelandic sweater) and follow the tracks of a white fox to Reykjavik, Iceland—where, centuries ago, Viking explorer Ingólfr Arnarson, the city's first inhabitant, dipped his weary feet in the Blue Lagoon before declaring his travels were over. Who wouldn't want to soak in a hot bath under the polar lights?

lupine flower

Árbær Open Air Museum

Arctic thyme tea

Arctic thyme

Thjodveldisbaerinn Stong

elf school

Dómskirkja

Parliament House

elf figurines

Thufa

whale watching

Old Harbour area

sea lion

narwhal

Khufu ship

caravan

papyrus

CAIRO

ful medames

falafel

The ancient city of Cairo is situated in the middle of an arid desert—where each drop of water is as valuable as forty camels. It's a place of pyramids thousands of years old, sphinxes with mysterious smiles, and tangled hieroglyphics. It's home to camels, donkeys, cats—both alive and mummified—and people who make their days more pleasant by sipping hot tea!

hieroglyphics

mummy

Tutankhamun

stuffed pigeon

simit bread

hibiscus tea

pottery

Manshiyat Naser (Garbage City)

Old Cairo

Khan el-Khalili bazaar

Street of Tentmakers

Mosque of al-Hakim

Pyramids at Giza

Sphinx

Citadel

Mosque of al-Azhar

camels

tuk-tuk

City of the Dead

shish taouk

Horus amulet

donkey

pharaoh figurine

Egyptian museum

lotus

cats

Faiyum oasis

Bab Zuweila gate

Al-Andalus garden

Cairo Tower

cruises on the Nile

27

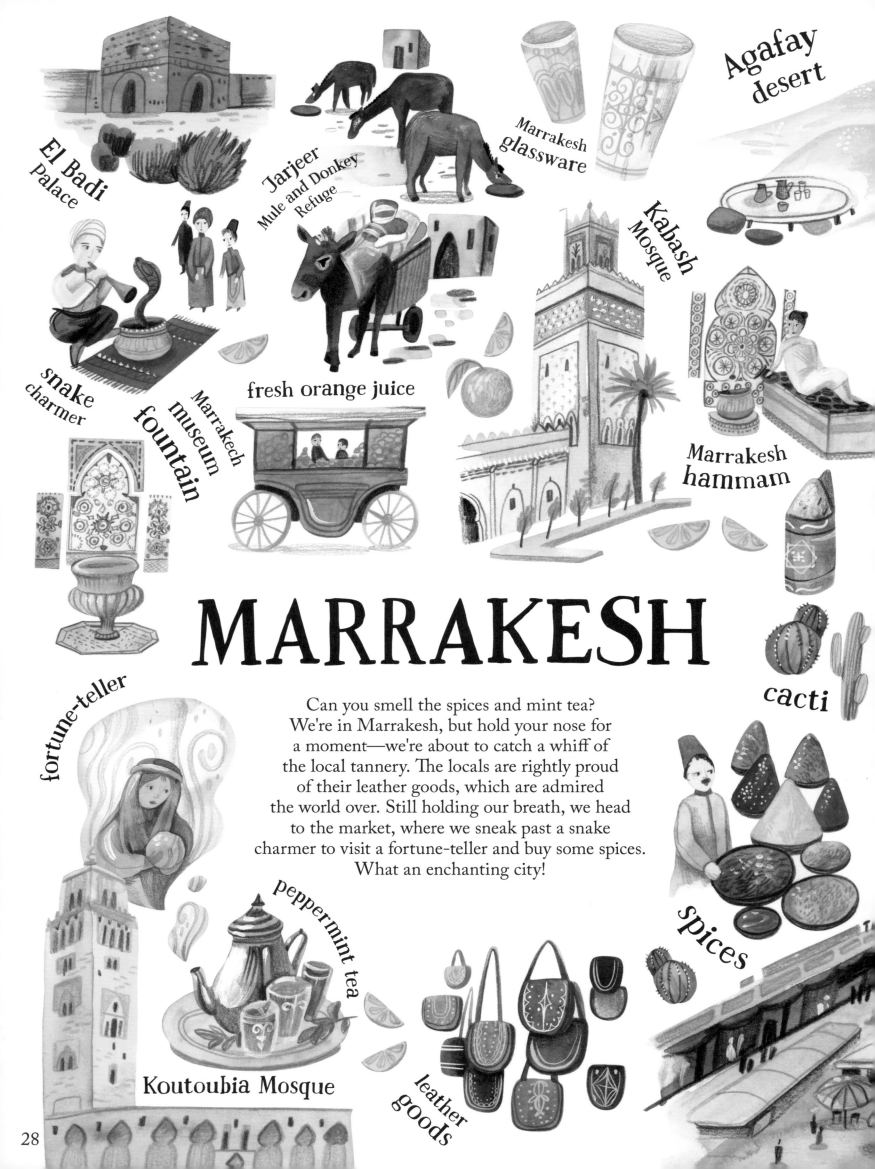

El Badi Palace

Jarjeer Mule and Donkey Refuge

Marrakesh glassware

Agafay desert

snake charmer

Marrakech museum fountain

fresh orange juice

Kabash Mosque

Marrakesh hammam

MARRAKESH

cacti

fortune-teller

Can you smell the spices and mint tea?
We're in Marrakesh, but hold your nose for
a moment—we're about to catch a whiff of
the local tannery. The locals are rightly proud
of their leather goods, which are admired
the world over. Still holding our breath, we head
to the market, where we sneak past a snake
charmer to visit a fortune-teller and buy some spices.
What an enchanting city!

spices

peppermint tea

Koutoubia Mosque

leather goods

Cactus Thiemann cactus garden

Moroccan lamps

André Heller's Anima Garden

Moroccan brass lamp

New Town Tree sculpture

Dar Si Said Museum

Marrakesh slippers

tagine

Marrakesh Berber carpets

Bab Agnaou Gate

babbouche

Marrakesh tanneries

Majorelle Gardens

Marrakesh Old Medina

Dyers souk

Zellige tilling

29

Aqueduct **of Valens**

Topkapi Palace

Kaiser Wilhelm Fountain

belly dancer

Tombili the cat

1513 Turkish world map

ISTANBUL

Dust off that old Persian rug and plop down—ideally cross-legged. Maybe it'll transform into a new, magical one and take you off to distant Istanbul, the city of the folk tales of *One Thousand and One Nights*, once the home of sultans. Join them in tasting roasted chestnuts and dream of Eastern scents under a silver crescent moon.

roasted chestnuts

seagulls

Blue Mosque

Turkish breakfast

baklava

Döner kebab

manti dumplings

sultan

pide

Cağ kebab

Spoonmaker's **Diamond**

Turkish coffee

çay

Dancing Fountain of Sultan Ahmed

stuffed mussels

Dolmabahçe Palace

Bosphorus Bridge

persian carpets

Rumeli fortress

Galata Tower

Beyoğlu district

Chora Church

Grand Bazaar

Hippodrome

Church of St. Anthony of Padua

Galatasaray tram

spice bazaar

tilework at Rüstem Pasha Mosque

dondurma – Turkish ice cream

Turkish ceramics

Golden Horn chain

fish market

Turkish baths

Kanyon Shopping Mall

Fener and Balat neighborhoods

Hagia Sophia

31

Tower of David

Natalie Portman

Monastery of St George of Choziba

King Solomon

Sibyl

Mount of Remembrance

rabbi

Jewish culture

Golden Menorah

wine

hummus

pomegranate juice

knafeh

Jerusalem bagel

sabich

Knesset Menorah

Zion Gate

JERUSALEM

halva

Step inside the Dome of the Rock, a holy site for Jews, Christians, and Muslims alike. Can you hear the learned rabbis quietly reading the Torah scrolls? Humble pilgrims from all over the world come in silence, heading for the Wailing Wall with a paper containing a secret wish. They slip it between the stones, believing that their wish will be granted.

Israeli salad

Church of Mary Magdalene

The Last Supper

Jewish Quarter

Mount of Olives

Montefiore Windmill

Dome of the Rock

poppy anemone

pilgrim

Church of the Holy Sepulchre

Tomb of Jesus

Damascus Gate

Via Dolorosa

Hebrew music

Garden Tomb

Garden of Gethsemane

David's Tomb

gazelles

Biblical Zoo

Israel Museum

Soreq Cave

Yemin Moshe neighborhood

Wailing Wall

Shrine of the Book

Church of the Dormition

33

Lantern Festival

Old Beijing paper-cut

Chaoyang Theatre acrobats

South China tiger

kung fu

Shidu Nature Park

addax

Panda House

bamboo

Great Wall of China

Chinese knots

red panda

Purple Bamboo Park

jade dragon

BEIJING

Wander along the Great Wall of China winding
for thousands of miles across the country—so long
it's visible from outer space! In ancient times,
it protected Beijing from invasion. At the city's
heart lies the emperor's Forbidden City—once
off-limits, now open for all to see in all its glory
and guarded by nine pairs of dragon's eyes.
Our waving cat is wishing us good luck!

slide at Great Wall of China

Gubei Water Town

Old Summer Palace

Beijing cheongsam

Mutianyu section of the Great Wall

Temple of Heaven

National Grand Theatre

Guanmiao Pavilion in Jingshan Park

Seventeen-Arch Bridge

Nine-Dragon Wall

Forbidden City

Panjiayuan Antique Market

pea-flour cake

Beijing high-speed train

jasmine tea

Pearl Market

Zhajiangmian noodles

Quingyan Stone Boat

Dragon Boat Festival

Chinese lucky cat

Chinese dumplings

tanghulu

Amazing Robots of Wu Yulu

Peking duck

aiwowo

weiqi

China Watermelon Museum

White Pagoda

Beijing Olympic Tower

Beihai Park

plum blossom

table tennis

Beijing Olympic Museum

35

Chunar Fort

Sarnath

Nepali temple

Mulagandha Kuti Vihar

Shri Kashi
Vishwanath temple

entrance

Darbhanga Ghat

to Vishalakshi temple

Dashashwamedh Ghat

Leaning Temple of Varanasi

wish candles

River Ganges

Ganga Aarti ritual

pashmina

sari-making

morning yoga

Varanasi market

floral wreaths

sari

wooden elephant

bracelets

henna tattoo

36

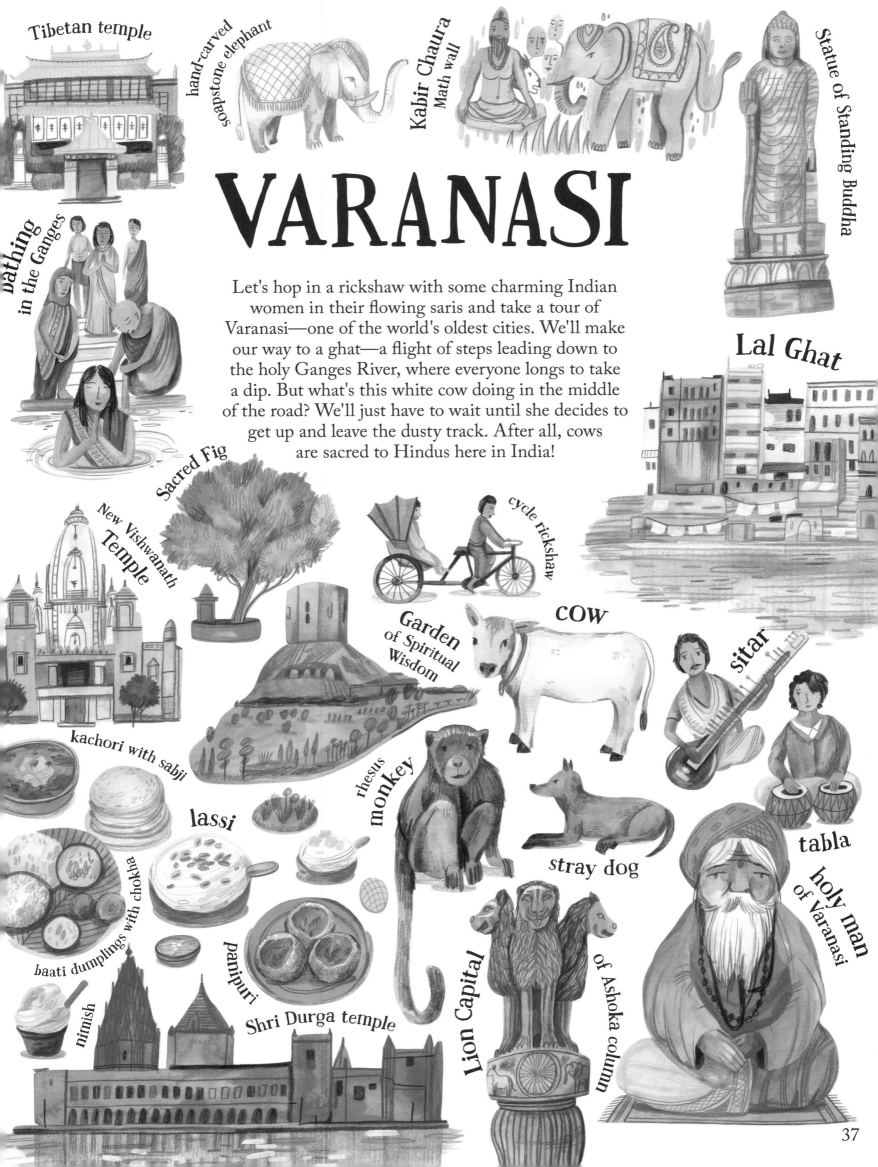

Tibetan temple

hand-carved soapstone elephant

Kabir Chaura
Math wall

Statue of Standing Buddha

VARANASI

bathing in the Ganges

Let's hop in a rickshaw with some charming Indian women in their flowing saris and take a tour of Varanasi—one of the world's oldest cities. We'll make our way to a ghat—a flight of steps leading down to the holy Ganges River, where everyone longs to take a dip. But what's this white cow doing in the middle of the road? We'll just have to wait until she decides to get up and leave the dusty track. After all, cows are sacred to Hindus here in India!

Lal Ghat

Sacred Fig

New Vishwanath Temple

cycle rickshaw

Garden of Spiritual Wisdom

cow

sitar

kachori with sabji

rhesus monkey

stray dog

tabla

lassi

holy man of Varanasi

baati dumplings with chokha

nimish

panipuri

Shri Durga temple

Lion Capital

of Ashoka column

golden shower flower

durian

elephant

khlong boat

Suan Pakkad museum

Asian vine snake

Pink Ganesha statue

Wat Bowonniwet Vihara

Chatuchak weekend market

Grand Palace

Thai silk

Buddha heads

BANGKOK

Bang Royal

Pa-In Palace

Emerald Buddha

Hop in a tuk-tuk for an exciting ride around the city! Buddhas big and small, made of stone, gold, or even flesh and bone—all are welcome in Bangkok! Don't forget to check out the "floating market," where you can find fresh veggies and, if you're feeling brave, a scorpion skewer—a local delicacy.

Bang Krachao park

muay thai

puppet theater in the Artist's House

King Rama IX Park

Wat Paknam Bhasicharoen

Baiyoke sky tower

Khao San Road

Sri Maha Mariamann temple

Erawan museum

Thai massage

street food

fried scorpion on a skewer

tuk-tuks

Wat Pho

royal barge

Damnoen Saduak floating market

Maeklong railway market

Wat Arun

butterfly pea flower tea

pad thai

mango sticky rice

volcano drink

tom yum

som-tum

39

banyan fig tree

Ta Prohm temple

romduol flower

Angkor Wat

Ta Som temple

Angkor Thom

Angkor silk farm

Cambodian dancers

Srah Srang lake

Buddhist monk

Terrace of the Leper King

fish spa pedicure

wood carving at Artisans Angkor

Khmer cakes

Phare Cicrus acrobats

Phnom Bok temple

Khal Spean waterfall

rice wine

Siem Reap River

prahok ktiss

red ant beef salad

fish amok

lok lak

sticky rice in bamboo

40

bananas

jeep tour

Phnom Kulen
waterfall

Preah Vihear
temple

elephants

Banteay Srey
Butterfly Centre

Banteay Srei

Psar Chaa
market

Crocodile
Farm

golden lion tamarin

War Museum
of Cambodia

SIEM REAP

Banksei
Chamkrong

Deep in the Cambodian jungle, not far from
the vibrant city of Siem Reap, lies the ancient
Angkor Wat temple, where the roots of fig trees
have overtaken everything. Down by the nearby
river, the local fishermen calmly eat their red-ant
salads, while indulging in a proper fish pedicure.

floating villages

Prek Toal bird sanctuary

fishermen's huts

Tonle Sap
lake

roseate
spoonbill

HOI AN

Experience the charm of Hoi An, Vietnam—a blooming city of lotuses, where nimble swallows dart among the clouds and boats hung with colorful lanterns bob gently by the Old Quarter waterfront. Every Vietnamese fisherman knows Hoi An, so why not do some fishing? Your help with the rice harvest in irrigated fields—wear flip-flops, if you like!—would be much appreciated. The locals may reward you with a ride on a water buffalo . . .

Central market

fish market

nón lá hat

Vietnamese flip-flops

Hoi Quan Hai Nam

Wall Street dressmaker

silk moth

Hoi An Silk Village

Thanh Hà Pottery Village

mask carved from a tree root

Âu Lac Wood Art

King Bong Carpentry Village

silk fabrics

golden dragon

hibiscus

white-throated kingfisher

barn swallow

Chinese guardian lion

Chàm Islands

tailorbird

An Bang Beach

snorkeling

floating lotus lights

coral reefs

paper
lanterns

green tea

sugar cane
juice

paddling at sunset

Cao lâu

Pho Bo

Vietnamese
iced coffee

Phuoc Lam Pagoda

Hoi An
dancers

Phuoc Kien
Assembly Hall

bánh mì

spring rolls

seared tuna

Japanese
Bridge

Old Quarter

white rose dumplings

cycle
rickshaw

cycling

Tra Nhieu
Fishing Village

Thu Bon River

temple bells
in Hoi An Museum

Water Puppet Theater

Bay Mau
Coconut Forest

lotus
flower

water buffalo
riding

growing rice

Kyo folding fan

Iwatayama Monkey Park

Kyoto Railway Museum

Daigoji temple

KYOTO

Arashiyama bamboo grove

Is this a dream? It's like being in the middle of a Japanese garden . . . Charming geisha patter along the Philosopher's Walk in lovely zori sandals, sighing softly into the breeze of their fans. *How lovely it is under the cherry blossom,* they think. Meanwhile, the plucking of the silk-stringed koto fills the air with soothing music that even the deer and red pandas seem to be enjoying.

red panda

Sagano railway

Okazaki Shrine

kimekomi doll

Nijo Castle

pickles at Nishiki market

Sanzen-in temple

Kokedara moss garden

Japanese garden

Kinkaku-ji temple

44

onsen (Kyoto hot springs)

Minami-za theater

pagoda at Kiyomizu-dera Temple

Toji Temple

Byodo-In temple

sushi

sakura

nama-fu

ramen

koto, the Japanese harp

matcha desserts

Philosopher's Walk

kiyomizu yaki

tea ceremony

matcha tea

Fushimi Inari-taisha shrine

paper umbrella

yatsuhashi

geisha

torii gates

45

Three sisters

Blue Mountains Botanic Garden

Watson's Bay

Wollemi pine

North Head

Captain James Cook

rugby

water dragon

Sydney Observatory

yellowfin tuna

John Dory

Koala Park Sanctuary

Badu Mangroves

Sydney rock oysters

Australian king prawns

Sydney Town Hall

Taronga Zoo

fish market

Paddington

Sydney Harbour Bridge

Sydney Harbour

46

Festival of the Winds

The Domain

Hyde Park

pygmy possum

Queen Victoria Building

SYDNEY

Visit the ultra-modern Australian city of Sydney once and you'll be returning in your mind over and over—like a human boomerang. You'll fondly recall concerts at the Opera House, sleek bridges, delicious avocado toast, and swimming in a pool where the surface meets the ocean. A single dive will get you there! You can practice your jumps, especially the high and long ones, at the local zoo—just copy the kangaroos!

Bondi Baths

kangaroo

high tea

avocado toast

cricket

Bondi Park

Sydney Tower

Sea Life Aquarium

Anzac biscuits

surfing

Art Gallery of New South Wales

The Rocks historic area

boomerang

Aboriginal carving of a whale

sailing ship in Sydney Harbour

We gratefully acknowledge that Sydney stands upon the homelands of the Eora and the Dharug, Indigenous peoples who have an enduring connection to this place despite being forcibly displaced by European colonization.

Statue of Liberty

Flatiron Building

Empire State Building

Chrysler Building

Central Park

ice skating at Rockefeller Center

Thanksgiving

Times Square

chipmunk

raccoon

Greenwich Village

Federal Hall

Manhattan Bridge

Harlem

St. Patrick's Cathedral

cereal

NYC milkshake

hot dogs

food truck

I ♥ NY
logo by Milton Glaser

cronut

club sandwich

NYC-style cheesecake

street art

hip hop

black-and-white cookies

donuts

pastrami sandwich

MIAMI

Finally, a place to kick back, put on your sunglasses, and witness the most beautiful sunrise in the world! No surprise that everyone who visits Miami does so to unwind—this city of sun-soaked beaches, deep-blue waves, and swaying palm trees has the perfect vacation vibe. Cruise around in a Cadillac, indulge in a slice of key lime pie, or dive down to a shipwreck. Miami has much to offer, from the top of the Freedom Tower to the bottom of the Atlantic Ocean!

Collins Avenue

Collins Av

Skyview Miami Observation wheel

Cape Florida Lighthouse

basketball

MIAMI 5

Historic Virginia Key Beach Park

Miami sunset

Española Way

old Florida bus

Calle 8

deep sea fishing boat

sailboat

Little Havana

zombie palm

jade vine

surfing

Miami Beach

We gratefully acknowledge that Miami stands upon the homelands of the Tequesta, the Ohlone, the Ramaytush, and the Muwekma, Indigenous peoples who have an enduring connection to this place despite being forcibly displaced by European colonization.

wild parrots of Telegraph Hill

Transamerican Pyramid

Maya Angelou

jeans

Steve Jobs

Dolores Park

popsicles

first jukebox

Janis Joplin

martini

Sillicon Valley

hippie movement

Dungeness crab

San Francisco Botanical Garden

balloon trips

dahlia

Oracle Park

Osher Rainforest

Golden Gate Bridge

Golden Gate ferry

Fort Alcatraz

Maritime Historical Park

San Francisco cable cars

steep roads

Twin Peaks

Wood Line

Lombard Street

Alamo Square

Ghiardelli hot fudge sundae

tiny yellow GoCars

16th Avenue Tiled Steps

Chinatown

Castro District

SAN FRANCISCO

Zoom across the Golden Gate Bridge in a flowery hippie bus—*Yahoo! No, help! Stop!* Taking a drive down Lombard Street is like riding a rollercoaster. And look at those colorful balloons bobbing in the air. So many amazing things originated in San Francisco—popsicles, jeans, the jukebox, to name a few. Such imaginative surroundings produce brilliant people—Steve Jobs and Maya Angelou among them.

The "Long Now" Orrery: a 10,000-year clock

sailing

sea lions at Pier 39

PIER 39

Seward Street Slides

Land's End

We gratefully acknowledge that San Francisco stands upon the homelands of the Ohlone, the Ramaytush, and the Muwekma, Indigenous peoples who have an enduring connection to this place despite being forcibly displaced by European colonization.

NEW ORLEANS

brown pelican

Tree of life

white magnolia

golf

streetcars

Louis Armstrong

his trumpet

The tranquil city of New Orleans lies on the winding banks of the Mississippi River, right in the middle of valley swamps inhabited by terrifying alligators. It's the cradle of jazz—listen to Louis Armstrong and sing along to the rhythm of his trumpet. Then treat yourself to some delicious beignets.

French street musicians

New Orleans Pharmacy Museum

Treme's Petit Jazz Museum

jazz band

cotton candy

Faubourg Marigny

Magazine Street

jazz festivals

cats

luna moth

swamps

alligator watching tour

City Park

alligator

We gratefully acknowledge that New Orleans stands upon the homelands of the Chahta Yakni (Choctaw) and the Chitimacha, Indigenous peoples who have an enduring connection to this place despite being forcibly displaced by European colonization.

Sky Railway

skiing

Kasha-Katuwe Tent Rocks

American bison

Santa Fe National Forest

La Cieneguilla petroglyph

Zuni amulet

glass blowing

Pueblo and Ute people

Museum of International Folk Art

traditional ceramics

low adobe houses

Santa Fe style rug

Indian market

coreopsis

agastache

Museum of New Mexico

Western diamond rattlesnake

pueblos

We gratefully acknowledge that Santa Fe stands upon the homelands of the Pueblos and the Núu-agha-tʉvʉ-pʉ (Ute), Indigenous peoples who have an enduring connection to this place despite being forcibly displaced by European colonization.

57

poutine

West Coast oysters

seaplane tour

English Bay

salmon candy

whale watching

Kitsilamo Beach

Vancouver Maritime Museum

California rolls

kayaking

Pacific dogwood flower

Haida and Kwakiutl masks

Olympic cauldron

Stevenson fishing village

Lighthouse Park

totem pole

dugout canoe

Museum of Anthropology

hockey

Gastown steam clock

VANCOUVER

Ilanaaq
cairns made by the Inuit Inukshuk

We strenuously paddle our kayak all around
Vancouver, Canada—land of the maple
leaf—toward beavers, otters, and delicious maple
syrup. After a quick break, we strap on our skis
and zoom down Grouse Mountain, giving it our all!
But we're overtaken by a dog sled.
That was fun, now let's go do some fishing!

VanDusen
Botanical Garden

totem pole

Brockton Point

horse-drown tour
at Stanley Park

Lions

maple leaves

maple syrup

Canada Place

Science Museum

West End

Vancouver City Hall

Marine Building

Brockton Point Lighthouse

Queen Elizabeth Park

aquabus

SkyBridge to Richmond

GRANVILLE ISLAND PUBLIC MARKET

Granville Island

Granville Street Bridge

SkyTrain

beaver

Sea to Sky Gondola

Otter

skunk

Capilano Suspension Bridge

fishing

Brittania Mine Museum

skiing down Grouse Mountain

Lumberman's Arch

dogsledding

We gratefully acknowledge that Vancouver stands upon the homelands of the Cayuse, Umatilla, and Walla Walla; the S'ólh Téméxw (Stó:lō); the Hul'qumi'num Treaty Group; the səl̓ilwətaʔɫ təməxʷ (Tsleil-Waututh); the šxʷməθkʷəy̓əmaʔɫ təməxʷ (Musqueam); the Skwxwú7mesh-ulh Temíxw (Squamish); and the Stz'uminus, Indigenous peoples who have an enduring connection to this place despite being forcibly displaced by European colonization.

59

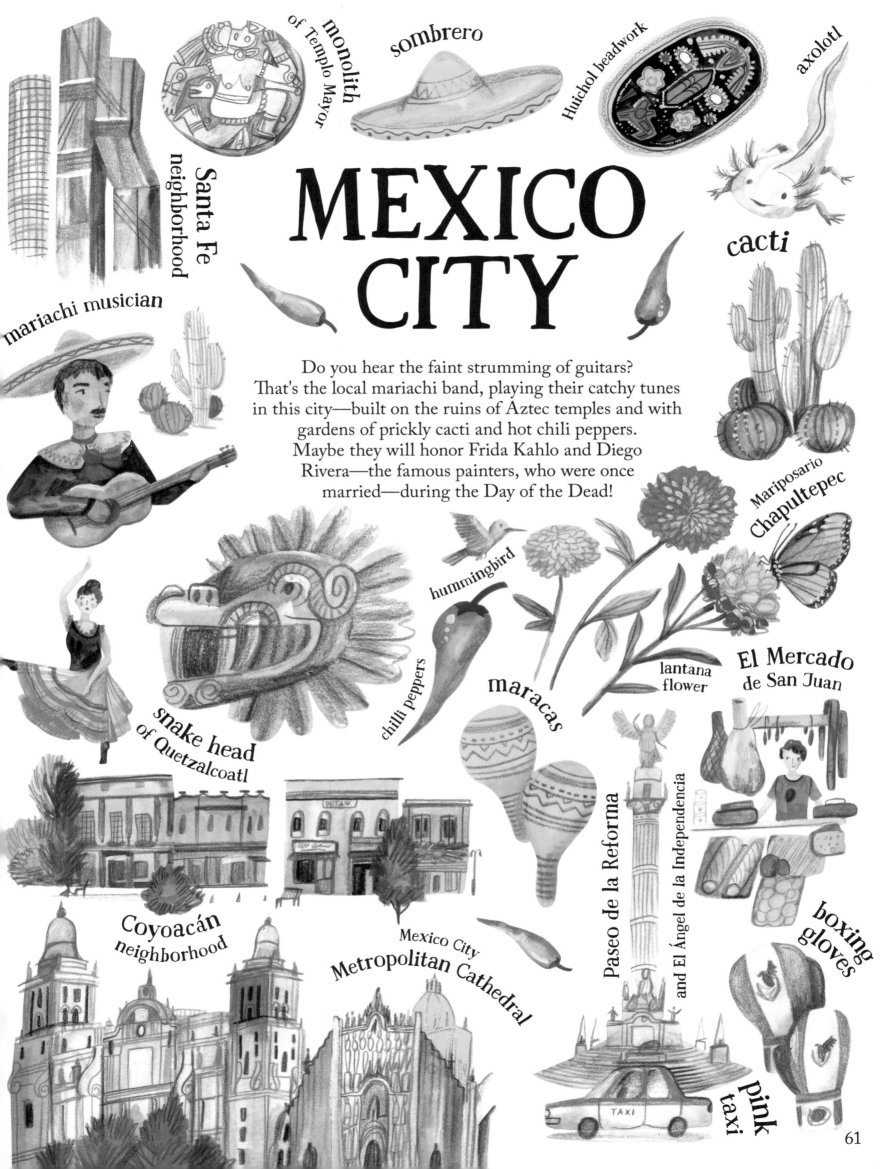

MEXICO CITY

Do you hear the faint strumming of guitars? That's the local mariachi band, playing their catchy tunes in this city—built on the ruins of Aztec temples and with gardens of prickly cacti and hot chili peppers. Maybe they will honor Frida Kahlo and Diego Rivera—the famous painters, who were once married—during the Day of the Dead!

monolith of Templo Mayor

sombrero

Huichol beadwork

axolotl

cacti

Santa Fe neighborhood

mariachi musician

Mariposario Chapultepec

hummingbird

snake head of Quetzalcoatl

chilli peppers

maracas

lantana flower

El Mercado de San Juan

Coyoacán neighborhood

Mexico City Metropolitan Cathedral

Paseo de la Reforma and El Ángel de la Independencia

boxing gloves

pink taxi

61

Cascatinha
Taunay waterfall

Dedo de Deus peak

Arpoador rock

Feira Hippie de Ipanema market

Rio Carnival

fireworks

Cathedral of Saint Sebastian

Arcos da Lapa

capuchin monkey

samba dancers

toucan

RIO DE JANEIRO

Ronaldo

football

Let's hit the road to Carnival! We're heading to Rio, where the toucan feathers are just as colorful as the costumes of the lively samba dancers. You'll be joining in too—it's contagious and the steps are easy. After a day of dancing, there's no better way to quench your thirst than with some delicious coconut water.

boa constrictor

agouti

Maracanã Stadium

Ilha Fiscal

Largo do Boticário square

hang-gliding

Sugarloaf Mountain

cableway on Sugarloaf Mountain

sightseeing by helicopter

Christ the Redeemer statue

Tijuca National Park

rock-climbing

Rodrigo de Freitas Lagoon

Las Etnias mural by Eduardo Cobra

Rocinha favela

Paulo Coelho

ALCHEMIST

Parque Lage mansion

AquaRio marine aquarium

coconut water

caipirinha

Selaron steps

yerba mate

Theatro Municipal Opera house

Copacabana Beach

açaí bowl

churrasco

brigadeiro

surfing

For more info, check out the following websites:

www.atlasobscura.com
www.earthtrekkers.com
fullsuitcase.com
inspiredbymaps.com
www.justapack.com
www.lonelyplanet.com
www.planetware.com
www.thecrazytourist.com
www.theculturetrip.com
thingstodoeverywhere.com
www.thrillophilia.com
www.timeout.com
www.touropia.com
travellersworldwide.com
www.tripadvisor.com

© B4U Publishing for Albatros, an imprint of Albatros Media Group, 2023
5. května 1746/22, Prague 4, Czech Republic
Author: Jana Sedláčková
Illustrator: Magdalena Konečná
Translator: Andrew Oakland
Editor: Scott Alexander Jones

Printed in China by Leo Paper Group

albatros